MW00938707

HOW WILL I ACHIEVE MY GOALS?

Six Simple Steps to Proven Success

Regina R. Carver

BALBOA PRESS

A DIVISION OF HAY HOUSE

Copyright © 2015 Regina R. Carver

Book Cover Design and Interior Illustrations:
Rob Allen @ n23art

All rights reserved. No part of this book may be used or reproduced by any means, graphic, electronic, or mechanical, including photocopying, recording, taping or by any information storage retrieval system without the written permission of the author except in the case of brief quotations embodied in critical articles and reviews.

Balboa Press books may be ordered through booksellers or by contacting:

Balboa Press
A Division of Hay House
1663 Liberty Drive
Bloomington, IN 47403
www.balboapress.com
1 (877) 407-4847

Because of the dynamic nature of the Internet, any web addresses or links contained in this book may have changed since publication and may no longer be valid. The views expressed in this work are solely those of the author and do not necessarily reflect the views of the publisher, and the publisher hereby disclaims any responsibility for them.

The author of this book does not dispense medical advice or prescribe the use of any technique as a form of treatment for physical, emotional, or medical problems without the advice of a physician, either directly or indirectly. The intent of the author is only to offer information of a general nature to help you in your quest for emotional and spiritual well-being. In the event you use any of the information in this book for yourself, which is your constitutional right, the author and the publisher assume no responsibility for your actions.

Print information available on the last page.

ISBN: 978-1-5043-3708-3 (sc)
ISBN: 978-1-5043-3709-0 (hc)
ISBN: 978-1-5043-3707-6 (e)

Library of Congress Control Number: 2015911255

Balboa Press rev. date: 08/28/2015

In Loving Memory of my parents,
Everett I. and Rosie L. Carver,
and my brother, Garry I. Carver

May you rest in peace

Making an effort is the firm
foundation of your success.

You are worth the effort.

CONTENTS

PREFACE

Thank you for choosing to pick up this book!! I am excited about our individual journey crossing paths in such a way that we are supporting one another. You will find something here to support you on your path to achieving your goals. By you reading this book, you are absolutely supporting my goal of providing encouragement on your journey to achieving your goals. Regardless of your unique way of doing things, your modus operandi, you will find a simple process to keep you motivated along the way.

The number of goals I've set over the years could rival the length of a very entertaining novel. I achieved some goals while others fell along the wayside and never materialized. Sound familiar? Maybe it's that reoccurring goal that never quite comes to fruition that is your concern. Help is here.

For me, one common thread in the success and failure of those goals was my conscious choice either to make an effort or give up. Sometimes I made an effort to figure out what to do, and things worked out. When I scrapped a goal and didn't act at all, the goal had no chance of coming to life. In the end, it really was up to me. I had to make a conscious effort to achieve what I wanted to see.

Using the *Six Simple Steps to Proven Success* outlined in this book made achieving my goals much easier to navigate. I particularly used the steps to complete the writing of this book. When I got stuck and had a bad case of writer's block, I used it. When I wasn't as motivated to write as I thought I should be, I used it. It helped to keep me making an effort in the right direction. This unique process was created from a combination of my past work experience, educational background, personal life experiences, life coaching experiences, the joy of encouraging others, and trial and error.

Most of all, my goal is to help you realize you can *be* and *have* what you set as your goal when you actually *do*—that is, when you make a conscious effort, no matter your circumstance. You have amazing power already in you.

Let's assume you have already decided on your goal. As you think about that goal, here are some assumptions to embrace that will help you take advantage of the support you will receive in the following pages:

- You have an idea of what you want to accomplish.

- You are ready to make the effort necessary to achieve your goal.

- You are looking for momentum that will allow you to consistently and confidently keep moving wisely toward your goal.

- You are flexible and willing to make changes on your road to achieving your goal.

- You can imagine yourself living your achieved goal now.

Isn't it good to know that the effort you have already made to read *How Will I Achieve My Goals?: Six Simple Steps to Proven Success* is increasing your chance of learning techniques to support your success? Making a conscious effort gives you confidence. Right now, you are reading what my effort produced. What can your effort produce? Help is on the way. Keep reading.

INTRODUCTION

How Will I Achieve My Goals?: Six Simple Steps to Proven Success was partly inspired by Rudine Howard (1964–1996). Rudine was a guest on *The Oprah Winfrey Show* about twenty years ago who had been diagnosed with anorexia nervosa. Actress Tracey Gold was also on the show as someone who had overcome the illness.

I remember Rudine asking Tracey how she had won the battle. I can still see her innocent face emanating sincerity as she asked; *How?* Tracey seemed to do her best to encourage Rudine.

Rudine's simple question left an indelible impression on me. *If only Rudine knew how.* She sat there with a life-threatening illness, and she simply wanted to know how she could overcome it. The *how* seemed to be my challenge at times too. This is where I often found myself stuck at the crossroad of *how* and effort.

At some time in your life, you may have wanted to achieve a goal and didn't know *how* to proceed. The path to meeting your goal may have appeared to be easy, but you were unable to achieve the goal. *How Will I Achieve My Goals?: Six Simple Steps to Proven Success* will help you along your way by showing you *how* to consistently determine a conscious effort and move forward.

How to get the best results from *How Will I Achieve My Goals?: Six Simple Steps to Proven Success*

Take time to read through the entire book, getting familiar with each step. As you read it, you will become both familiar and comfortable with the steps. There is power in being able to SEE your thoughts. One important activity in the book is taking time to write down your thoughts. Grab a journal. Write in this book where appropriate and possible. Type in a note pad, kind of electronic program. Do what works for you. Capture your thoughts in a format that you can review. Writing things down can give you the fuel to make an effort toward your goals, since this action has the power to strengthen your vision in your mind's eye. *How Will I Achieve My Goals?: Six Simple Steps to Proven Success* is designed to be an easy, quick read; it has the power to positively change your life and ideas on what it means to make an effort in any situation. There are all kinds of goodies here. Feel free to apply the six-step process to your own specific situation as you see appropriate. Choose what works for you...what moves you closer to your goal.

Before we jump right into the process, let's first take a look at the subject of setting goals.

Goals
Goals
Goals
GOALS
GOALS
Goals
GOALS
Goals
Goals
GOALS
Goals
GOALS
GOALS
GOALS
GOALS
GOALS

CHAPTER 1

YOUR GOAL MIND,
YOUR GOLD MINE

You have made a decision to make changes in your life, right? Do you have a goal in mind? Here are a few examples:

Specific Attainable Goal	General Goal
I will write for one hour each day until I finish my book.	I will write more.
I will walk to the end of the block today.	I will walk more.
I will watch television for one hour after work.	I will control my television viewing.

1

For the writing of this book, I reserved at least one hour each day to just write. Sometime I had plenty to write. Sometime there wasn't as much progress, but the act of making this effort gave me a sense of moving toward my goal. You are reading my accomplished goal right now.

When you have a goal, you have something to aim for. Goals give you direction and help you decide where to expend your effort in order to have the best chance of actually achieving your goal. When you make a conscious effort, your *goal centered mind* produces your *gold mine.* That gold mine is the treasured goal you had in mind and achieved!

An example of a personalized goal could be, *I will complete business school by (fill in the date)* _____.
This book is focused on the *how*—how you can confidently make an effort to achieve your specific goal or appropriately modify your goal as needed.

Write your thoughts down as you consider your goal. Is your goal specific? Is your goal general? What does this reflection reveal for you?:

Notes

Notes

Remember to always be clear on your intention when you set your goal. (Intention will be discussed more in step 1.) Your intention will support you as you move toward accomplishing your goal. My intention for writing this book was to give you encouragement and a guide to that treasured gold mine, aka your accomplished goal.

To help you stay focused on achieving your goals, *How Will I Achieve My Goals?: Six Simple Steps to Proven Success* will guide you in remembering that a goal requires you to make an EFFORT:

Step 1 – **Establish** what your goal is and why you want it.

Step 2 – Determine whether your strategy **Fits** your goal.

Step 3 – Determine whether your goal is **Fulfilling.**

Step 4 – **Observe** your progress in achieving your goal.

Step 5 – Measure the **Result** of your efforts.

Step 6 – Set a **Time Limit** for achieving your goal.

There is one word in each step in the process that is the main focus for that designated step. Using the first letter in each of these words in their respective step, they spell the word EFFORT. EFFORT is a main ingredient to achieving your goals:

Step 1 – **E**stablish
Step 2 – **F**it
Step 3 – **F**ulfilling
Step 4 – **O**bserve
Step 5 – **R**esult
Step 6 – **T**ime Limit

Taking action is a way of describing making an effort. Your effort is the life you breathe into your goals. You can bring your goals to life. Each step of the process will be discussed in detail to keep you on track in making a conscious effort toward achieving your goal. As you use this book, it will serve as your mobile accountability partner, reference, and inspiration. You will have a way of checking in on how you are performing and what you may need to do to stay on course or to change course. You will get there.

At this point, you have been introduced to the *Six Simple Steps to Proven Success*. Now, keep going. Make an effort to read about and use the process. You have the power to transform your effort into your desired goal! You must always make an effort to move in the direction of your goal. By taking actions, goals have a better chance of coming to life. Do what you can now.

Let's move on to what happens after setting your goal, also referred to as a resolution at times. Step 1 of the *Six Simple Steps to Proven Success*. It will help you *establish* your foundation. Establishing a foundation gives you something firm to build upon as you start out. Remember to follow the steps in order. After reading through the process one time, be sure to apply each individual step to your particular situation accordingly.

Wouldn't it be awesome to take what you learn here and make this system a trusted guide as you pursue all kinds of goals? Imagine the possibilities. Anne reaches out to other women online and forms a supportive community for a mysterious illness. Jay and Samantha build a successful community-based business that inspires youth to believe their dreams can come true. A teenaged Patti buys her first car by creating and selling unique graphic art. Octogenarian Robert sets his intention on walking at least a mile each day.

My doubt and fear, among other things, about actually finishing this book would arise and sometimes impede my progress. Would I be able to communicate in a way that would resonate with anyone? The *Six Simple Steps to Proven Success* process turned out to be a tool I referred to in times when I was a bit stalled or stuck. When you use this process, the goals you set and achieve can be unlimited. There is always an effort to be made.

You have the power to transform your effort
into your desired goal!

STEP 1 - Establish

STEP 6
Time Limit

STEP 5
Result

STEP 4
Observe

STEP 3
Fulfilling

STEP 2
Fit

STEP 1
Establish

CHAPTER 2

STEP 1: ESTABLISH WHAT YOUR GOAL IS AND WHY YOU WANT IT

What Do You Want?

Simply put, what do you want? No matter when or where you start, you must start by figuring out what you want. Start where you are. Determine your start date. It's time to let your imagination roam free. Have fun here. This is *your* dream. This is *your* goal.

Stepping Into Your Goal Exercise

Read this paragraph for instructions on how to step into your goal, then lay the book aside and practice doing so. Try your goal on now. You can do this by getting in a relaxed state of mind. Find a quiet place where you will not be disturbed. You can sit or lie down, but be sure you're not so relaxed you fall asleep. You are about to experience the good feelings your goal will bring. Take a few deep breaths. Inhale filling your stomach and imagine it shaped like a plump pear. Hold it for a count of four. Exhale fully like a deflating balloon. Now take time to feel each part of your body relax. You can mentally name or focus on parts of your body from your toes to the top of your head, assisting the progression of your relaxation. When you feel your body taken over by this relaxed state, imagine that the date for your achieved goal has arrived. Imagine yourself stepping right into the picture of living your ideal goal. Imagine the colors, smells, tastes, body sensations and feelings associated with your achieved goal. Stay there and feel the whole experience of your goal fully realized. With your eyes still closed, step out of the picture you have imagined. Now, look at yourself in the picture in your mind's eye, being, doing, and having your goal. Enjoy this time. When you're ready, come back to the present moment by being aware of your breathing and physical body. Open your eyes when you're ready. Is there a big grin on your face? I hope so. You can feel good *now*. Feel free to tweak your goal while in this state too. Use this technique to support your efforts whenever you like.

You've now stepped into your goal and felt what it feels like to achieve the goal. Your end result that you imagined during this exercise will appear because you will learn what consistency in your effort generates. Making an effort is how you show faith in a goal you cannot see in the present. This is how you will achieve any goal you set. Be consistent in your effort, and you have an amazing chance to pull your goal right into a tangible form.

- How did achieving your goal make you feel?
- How was your life better because you achieved your goal?
- Was anyone else's life positively changed by you reaching your goal?
- Do you have a better idea of what you want now?

Contemplating these questions can further help you develop a clear picture of your goal, and feel a sense of achievement now. Feels good, doesn't? This good feeling can give you energy to keep moving forward too.

Morgan Freeman's character, Monty Wildhorn, in the movie *The Magic of Belle Isle* (2012) made a fascinating comment about imagination: "Imagination, the most powerful force ever made available to humankind." What are you doing with your imagination? Use your imagination as you see necessary, just as you did in the previous exercise by stepping into your goal. You absolutely have the power to establish your goal in the unlimited space in your mind and then bring it to life.

Take a moment to jot down ideas about what you want, helping to establish your goal:

Notes

Notes

When establishing your goal, keep in mind that it is important to *act now* because this is the only time you *can* act to affect your future. The present is a present because it is the only time when you can act to make changes in your life. No effort or action can be taken in the past. It's gone. No effort or action can be taken in the future. It hasn't arrived. However, you affect your future by what you do in the present. Now that's a real present. And it is a real privilege to be aware of the present moment to take action. What you do now is what matters. Decide to make an effort. Do it now. You will reap the benefits of your goal when you make an effort in the present moment. While engaged in the present moment, I found being in a calm state provided me the clarity to make wise decisions too.

Determine Your Intention

Why do you want to achieve the goal you determined? Make your *why* clear so you have a reason to persevere and set an established course of action. Your intention can keep you focused on making an effort toward your goal during the ebb and flow of life. Some days things will work like magic and everything falls in place. And some days you may get an extra dose of challenges. I remember stepping away from my computer and feeling stuck because I hadn't written anything I felt was valuable for that day, while writing this book. Being able to reflect on the *why* kept me motivated to make an effort toward the completion of this book: My *why* during the writing of this book, remains the same: to encourage you on your journey to achieving your goals. I still embrace my *why*. Another word to reflect on to keep you motivated is *because*. Say to yourself or out loud, "I want to achieve this goal of _____ because _____." Hey, I'm not saying it's going to always be an easy process. But knowing that the challenging times are part of the process is helpful as well. You can work through the challenges. You can learn from the challenges and be wiser because of them.

What Tools or Actions Will Help Establish Your Goal?

If your goal is to travel to Africa, you could establish your intention by creating a vision board. Start with a piece of paper or poster board. Paste pictures, art, words, and even small objects associated with your goal on your vision board. What would inspire your African adventure? The word *safari*? A photo of the beautiful people? The animals? The pyramids? The Sahara Desert? You get to decide what will encourage you as you create your masterpiece.

The vision board will serve as a visual motivation to realize your goal, your intention. Be sure to place it where you can see it every day to get your daily fix of that good feeling of inspiration. I find vision boards very useful in helping me maintain positive energy to keep striving. I even take pictures of them and put them on my smartphone, and computer as wallpaper.

Here are a few more suggestions to strengthen the establishment of your goal:

- You can give attention to your goal through your chosen spiritual or ritual practice. As mentioned earlier, the present moment is where you can take action. Sometimes taking a few deep breaths may do the trick to keep you rooted in the present moment by being aware of your breath. This is where you make an effort, the present moment. Maybe this could be a ritual for you.

- You can pray in your customary way, if this is appealing to you. My prayers often aren't very formal. Sometimes I ask for guidance. Sometimes it's just me voicing my gratitude for all the people, situations and things I sometimes take for granted in my life.

- Pay attention to the world around you. You never know when an answer may appear. It could come through a commercial on television. A stranger you meet at the local grocery store might share just what you need to hear to establish your goal. While spending time in nature, a beautiful scene may reveal insight. Be aware.

Establishing your goal and being clear on your intention is an excellent foundation for achieving your goal.

Some people may be able to start without a lot of hoopla or fanfare and that's just how they initiate achieving a goal. Some people need more of a kick start like doing some research. Neither way is right or wrong. What's important is to be flexible and willing to make adjustments along the way. Of course, you have your own unique way of doing what you do. What if you have to make your own path? For example, what if you establish your goal as inventing some type of device for the older generation of people to facilitate their continued independence at home? What do you think you would need to do to establish this goal? It's still important to make the right effort as you start on your journey.

How Much Energy Are You Willing to Exert to Achieve Your Goal?

At this point, you have an idea of what you need to do to achieve your goal. And you have information to help you determine how you can proceed in achieving it. You now have examples of *how* your goal can be achieved. What conscious effort can you make toward your specific goal?

On a scale from 1 to 10, with 1 being weak and 10 strong, how do you gauge your energy level? Your energy level is directly related to your determination. Imagine that your goal is to learn to play the piano. How much time and energy are you willing to give to learning? One hour per week? One hour per day? Knowing this will help you further establish your goal.

Do you need to adjust your effort by revisiting what you decided in step 1? If not, proceed to step 2.

You absolutely have the power to establish your
goal in the unlimited space in your mind,
and then bring it to life.

STEP 2 - Fit

STEP 6
Time Limit

STEP 5
Result

STEP 4
Observe

STEP 3
Fulfilling

STEP 2
Fit

STEP 1
Establish

CHAPTER 3

STEP 2: DETERMINE WHETHER YOUR STRATEGY FITS YOUR GOAL

Does Your Strategy Fit Your Overall Goal?

What is a strategy? It's your personalized blueprint for achieving your goal. Here are a couple of sample strategies:

A strategy for increasing walking time in twenty-eight days could look like this:

	Walking Minutes	Number of Times per Week	Total Number of Minutes for Week
Week 1	10	3	30
Week 2	20	3	60
Week 3	30	3	90
Week 4	40	3	120

A strategy for passing a class could look like this:

1. Be clear on what is necessary to pass the class.
2. Ask instructor and fellow classmates for help, if needed.
3. Study as much as needed (such as one hour per day or thirty minutes every other day).
4. Check assignments for accuracy.
5. Turn in all assignments on time.

You can now establish a strategy that fits you—a strategy that is doable and includes steps to get you to your ultimate goal. Sometimes breaking down a goal into smaller steps will keep you from becoming overwhelmed, at different times throughout the process. Like climbing a mountain, a couple of leaps are impossible to reach the top. Taking a few small steps will get you there.

In step 1, you saw yourself living your dream goal. Here in step 2, your strategy helps you along the path to your goal as you take steps to get there. Here's where you can set short- and long-term goals. If you want to learn to swim, a short-term goal may be to find places in your community that offer beginners' swimming lessons. Your long-term goal may be to swim five laps.

Does your goal fit you? If so, your time and effort will be used wisely and efficiently because you have established a direction toward your goal with your personalized strategy.

Determine What You Need to Do to Achieve Your Goal

What if after attempting to set up a strategy, you found you don't know what to do? If so, you will still need to determine what to do. Consider doing some research. Who is doing what you dream of doing or has already accomplished your goal? Is there a person or organization that could help you in your efforts toward achieving your goal? Do you feel you have enough knowledge to get started? Now, what can you do?

Say your goal is to become an entrepreneur. You could contact an SBDC (Small Business Development Center), which offers free mentoring and counseling to budding entrepreneurs and more. Is there a person or group via the Internet that allows you to access relevant information or will allow you to send an email to ask for information? Can you make contact through social media? Can you become a member of a trade association having pertinent information? Can you make a phone call to obtain advice? Can you barter your skills to help someone while you get the benefit of their skills? Can you seek a volunteer position in your area of interest? Amazingly, it seems you gain more help my helping others at times. Could reading a relevant magazine or newspaper provide the needed insight?

Research a role model. Does this person have a blog, for instance? Is there anyone in your area of interest that has written an autobiography giving insight on the road to meeting his or her goal? What can you learn from it? Do you know anyone personally that can serve as your role model or a teacher you could reach out to for help? Are there any successful neighborhood businesspeople you could take to lunch to pick their brain? Be creative. There is always an effort to be made, even to form your strategy. Again, do you feel you have enough knowledge to get started? Now, what can you do?

What efforts require assistance? Can you brainstorm with someone or a group? Maybe you like bird watching, and your goal is to do more of it. Can you start your own local group of birdwatchers? What strategy can you create to support your effort to move confidently and consistently toward your goal? All these activities ensure your strategy fits your goal.

Take time to write out your strategy. This will help make your goal more real and achievable. You will have an idea of what actions and efforts to make. Get it out of your head and on paper so you can review it. Be careful here. Make an effort to focus on your strategy. Make the plan. Refer to the earlier strategy examples presented in this chapter. Use them as a guide to keep yourself moving forward toward your goal.

Is Your Strategy Appropriate for Achieving Your Goal?

Let's say your strategy for driving the most direct route to work requires you to take the first left turn immediately after leaving home. If you decide to take the first right turn instead, this action would be contrary to supporting your goal. Like a cat hiding in the tall grass and focused on catching a bird, its prey, have a strategy that gives you the best chance of achieving your goal. Again, ensure your strategy fits your goal.

So do a reality check here. If your goal is to become a doctor, a strategy that includes taking the right classes and maintaining a certain GPA is appropriate. Neglecting your studies is an inappropriate action that will lead you on an indirect, arduous route. Be careful where you put your effort. Always make a conscious effort while making sure your strategy fits your goal.

How about stepping into your goal again as you did in step 1? Does your goal still fit? Does it fit like a glove?

Is your goal the fit you imagined
after creating your strategy?

⇒ Do you need to adjust your effort by revisiting what you decided in steps 1 and 2? If not, proceed to step 3.

Take time to write down ideas regarding your strategy toward your goal. What might be a good first step? One of my strategies for writing this book was creating an outline. I then had something to focus my attention on as I wrote. The outline gave me some direction and structure. I really had a sense of whether my strategy fit what I planned to achieve. What can you do as you create your strategy to give your goal focus and keep you on track?

Notes

Notes

STEP 3 - Fulfilling

STEP 6
Time Limit

STEP 5
Result

STEP 4
Observe

STEP 3
Fulfilling

STEP 2
Fit

STEP 1
Establish

CHAPTER 4

STEP 3: DETERMINE WHETHER YOUR GOAL IS FULFILLING

Is Your Goal Worth Your Effort?

Do you have a feeling of fulfillment when you think of achieving your goal? Listen to your gut feeling. Will there be a feeling of satisfaction and accomplishment? Great! Satisfaction surrounds your effort when you know your goal will be fulfilling and worth pursuing, right?

At this point, you've already created a strategy. You have an idea of the details like time, effort, finances needed through any research you conducted. As you move forward, making an effort, be sure to check to see if your reason is fulfilling enough to keep you motivated to achieve your goal. You decide what is fulfilling for you.

Is the Goal Your Idea or Someone Else's?

If the goal is not your idea, you may feel some resistance, sluggishness, uneasiness, or discomfort when making an effort. You can still achieve the goal. If it is not in alignment with your deepest intention, it might become a struggle. You may experience unnecessary problems on your journey to achieving your goal by taking this route. You may not feel that achieving the goal will fulfill your intention, when it is someone else's goal for you. Being fulfilled is best realized when you are true to yourself and what inspires you to make an effort. You have one of the best tools with you all the time to guide you. Your body. Yes, your body. Listen to its messages. What feelings, or body sensations do you experience when contemplating the fulfillment factor of your goal? Listen to the sensations in your body. The joy in your heart. The pain in your back. The feeling in your gut. Listen to these messages. What are they telling you? *I feel queasy when I think of this goal. I need to rethink this ...* for instance.

What If You Don't Feel Fulfilled by Pursuing Your Goal?

Maybe a closer analysis of your feelings and deeper intention is in order to bring peace and help you make an effort in the right direction—or make whatever efforts you deem necessary to be more in alignment with your goal. The alignment was a struggle for me. at times. My original outline for this book changed several times. After further analysis, I changed the outline to be more in alignment with conveying the message. Being in harmony with, being in cooperation with, being at peace with your goal can bring a feeling of satisfaction and fulfillment, which is your vehicle to move you forward.

Florence Scovel Shinn (1871–1940), author of *The Game of Life and How to Play It* and a new thought spiritual teacher, wrote, "He must be in harmony with a thing in order to attract it." Are you in harmony with your goal? Or are you feeling uneasy and in discord with it?

Isn't being in harmony with your goal an awesome image? Like dancing the perfect tango. If your effort is in harmony with achieving your goal, you will find your path becoming easier for you. You will find yourself totally enjoying the process because you'll find it is simple to focus on your goal and make an effort when your goal is fulfilling.

Is Your Goal Good for You and Others?

If your goal is not good for you and others, check your intention here. You could very well use your effort in a way that could be harmful to you and others.

A feeling of satisfaction surrounds
your efforts when you know
your goal will be fulfilling and worth pursuing, right?

⇒ Do you need to adjust your effort by revisiting what you decided in steps 1, 2 or 3? If not, proceed to step 4.

Take a few minutes to jot down some adjectives or phrases that remind you of how fulfilling you believe your goal will be (for example, brings peace to me and others, makes me happy, satisfies the need to bring my family together, provides housing to hundreds of children). You can keep this list as encouragement, which you'll probably need from time to time.

Notes

Notes

STEP 4 - Observe

STEP 6
Time Limit

STEP 5
Result

STEP 4
Observe

STEP 3
Fulfilling

STEP 2
Fit

STEP 1
Establish

CHAPTER 5

STEP 4: OBSERVE YOUR PROGRESS IN ACHIEVING YOUR GOAL

Is Your Effort Observable in Some Tangible Way?

Documenting your progress by tracking your effort is an excellent way to stay on track. You can simply use a pen and paper to keep track. Or use a flowchart; a wall calendar; a project-management app on your smartphone or tablet, or a program on your computer; or a voice recorder. Be creative. Design your own form, or use the one in this book as a guide. Here's an example:

Goal: Plan a vacation with spouse

Activity	Date	Notes
Determine the time frame		
Determine the budget		
Determine when planning needs to be complete		
Determine the destination		
Check out local activities to explore		
Make reservations for airfare		
Make reservations for hotel accommodations		
Rent car if necessary		

Goal: _____

Activity	Date	Notes

Adjust your efforts wherever needed. Sometimes you will need to change course along the way. What if you decided to run a marathon and didn't know where to start pursuing this adventure? You could Google how others started their journey. You could decide to start out walking at least a block, get a physical trainer, change your diet to provide the essential fuel you need, etc. However, you must consistently make an effort.

An accountability partner is helpful. Where possible, the arrangement reaps high dividends when both individuals present a goal for accountability. It is invested interest for each person. Pick someone you feel totally comfortable being open and honest about mutually sharing your journey. Having an individual to answer to can be motivating. I have an accountability partner and the arrangement works great to keep us both on track. Yes, we are on the honor system and no one is personally watching over us. But it really makes me kick into gear and make an effort when I know I have to at least take that small step I agreed to take. We have regularly scheduled check-in times. Accountability works for group efforts too!

A life coach could help you in your area of concern as well. Like the relationship between an athlete and coach; a life coach can help you strengthen your mental muscle to cross the goal line, pun intended. ☺ Coaches help bring out the power you already have within you.

I am a certified life coach, helping individuals make changes to fully share their unique gifts with the world. Hence, allowing the freedom to live life fully now. I studied in the coaching program of Martha Beck, PhD, bestselling author, and columnist for O, The Oprah Magazine. I also use the services of a life coach whenever necessary. There are all types of life coaches today, health and fitness, executive, spiritual, personal development, relationship, and the list goes on. There is even group coaching available.

Sidebar Break

We're just about halfway through the *Six Simple Steps to Proven Success*. Let's take a break from the steps of the process for straight talk here. You already have amazing power within you. This power does not discriminate. It is available to you. It is your choice to use this power to make an effort toward your chosen goal. What an awesome choice you have. Nothing happens for you until you think the thought, take the action, make the effort.

Direct your thoughts in the direction that supports you like the wind supporting the dance of a kite floating in the air on a windy, sunny autumn day. Ultimately, only you have control of your efforts. No one else. In order for anything to happen in your life, you have to make the effort. You control you. Your thoughts. Your feelings. Your attitude. You're in the driver's seat, with the controls in your hands. Your goal is within your control. Nothing happens until you take action, make the effort. From scratching an itch, to finding a job, to trying out for the baseball team, to going to the audition, to finding clients for your business, to graduating from college, to participating in the Yoga class, to being vulnerable and making yourself available for true love…all these events have one common denominator, YOU HAVE TO MAKE THE EFFORT.

In the book *Steering by Starlight: Find Your Right Life, No matter What!* by Martha Beck, PhD, I learned that identifying my style of taking action is conducive to helping me move confidently forward too. Ms. Beck referenced the four conative styles created by Kathy Kolbe. Those styles are Quick Start, Follow Thru, Fact Finder and Implementor. I am primarily a Fact Finder, which really comes in handy to help clarify the direction I take. Knowing my profile, helped me tremendously. I possess the other styles, but as a Fact Finder I also have a tendency to analyze information and sometimes miss taking actions to help keep me on track to achieving my goals. None of the styles are either good or bad. Knowing I may need to partner with someone that I see primarily as one of the other styles was freeing. Or being aware of when I may need to draw on one of the other styles in me, gives me confidence. For specific information about the Kolbe action styles, visit www.kolbe.com and click the *Why Kolbe* or *Assessments* tabs along the top of the page. Or just be mindful of how and when you tend to take action or make an effort toward your goal.

What if you observe your progress in step 4 and realize you're simply *stuck*? You're just not moving in any direction, even though you truly want to move toward your goal. Alice Boyes, PhD, offers additional strategies in her book *The Anxiety Toolkit: Strategies for Fine-Tuning Your Mind and Moving Past Your Stuck Points* like: Thinking Shifts to Overcome Excessive Hesitancy, Entertain the Idea That Your Actions Might Have Positive Consequences and Recognize the Value of Acting with Uncertainty. Remember there is always an effort to be made. If you're in a stuck mode, perhaps finding ways to deal with the situation could be helpful. Ms. Boyes presents great ideas on the topic of: *stuck.*

Again, only you have control of your efforts. You are responsible for setting and nurturing your goals. Remember this. Embrace this. You have to make it happen. This is your one and only beautiful and precious life. Make of it what you will.

Nice break, huh? Okay, now back to the process.

Continue Step 4: Observe Your Progress in Achieving Your Goal

You may have started to observe your efforts in step 2 as part of your strategy. Does your system to measure your progress provide a clear picture of where you stand? Somehow you must create a way to transform your progress into a visible form to observe. What you accomplish can then be clearly gauged so you know where you are on your journey. When you know where you are in the process, you can determine if it is worth continuing on the path. You can still get there, but it may require a turn or two. You have choices you can adjust while making an effort. What support or changes are needed as you observe your progress?

Observing and taking time to analyze what energy, time, and money you have invested can help you make the most prudent decisions for your success. Make decisions that support your goal. This awareness can be empowering. After observing your trackable, measurable progress, you may determine that more effort is required. Are you maximizing your effort? Twenty minutes a day? Thirty minutes a day? An hour three times a week? Do you need to make an effort to relax and be still or to set aside time to enjoy life and recharge your battery? Give yourself permission to do nothing if warranted. I found sometimes taking a break from my goal actually gave me more energy to keep moving forward more consistently. You may see that you are exerting too much effort in a particular area. You can adjust your effort based on your observations. Would a schedule be helpful? Would a schedule be helpful? Have you set a schedule to make an effort toward your goal? The following is a sample schedule and a blank schedule for your use, to help you observe your progress.

Goal Schedule For: Pass math class with a grade of an A

Date	Study Time	Y / N	Notes
	1 Hr		
	1 Hr		
	1 Hr		
	1 Hr		
	1 Hr		
	1 Hr		
	1 Hr		

Goal Schedule For: _____

Date	Time	Y / N	Notes

Again, step into your goal as instructed in step 1. Now step back and observe your current progress. Established? Fitting? Fulfilling? Take time to write your thoughts down regarding your progress and any adjustments you may have to make:

Notes

Notes

Are You Remaining True to Your Goal's Intent?

Now that you've observed your progress, are you being true to your intent by keeping your intent in mind? Keep your intent in mind or in written form where you can see it often. For example, you intend to become a teacher by a certain date so you can help inspire children in developing their special gifts. Or you intend to run a marathon by a certain date to improve your health. If you're not true to your intent, what good are your efforts? Is the goal still something you want to work toward? Take a look. Be clear here. As you observe your effort, you have more insight into your progress and what you need to do.

Can you see your effort producing your intended goal? Can you see your goal manifesting? Be sure your intention is driving your effort like a well-maintained car.

Somehow you must create a way to track your progress
so you can observe what you've accomplished
on your journey along the way.

⇒ Do you need to adjust your effort by revisiting what
you decided in steps 1, 2, 3 or 4? If not, proceed to step 5.

After observing your efforts in step 4, take time to jot down your thoughts on your intent. Is your intent strong enough to carry you to the finish line of achieving your goal?

Notes

STEP 5 - Result

GOAL!

STEP 6
Time Limit

STEP 5
Result

STEP 4
Observe

STEP 3
Fulfilling

STEP 2
Fit

STEP 1
Establish

CHAPTER 6

STEP 5: MEASURE THE RESULT OF YOUR EFFORTS

What Are You Producing?

Is your effort taking you toward the end result you established in step 1? Or is your result starting to look like an apple though your goal is to acquire an orange? If this is the case, your effort and your goal clearly are out of alignment. Plant the right seed of intention. You want to make the right effort toward what your goal was intended to produce, right?

What Is Your Final Outcome?

Keep your goal in focus. Even before the final outcome materializes, you must still track and measure your efforts, as discussed in step 4. Be aware that your efforts must be directed toward your desired result: your desired goal. Maintain concentration on the right efforts throughout the process. Imagine accidentally putting your effort into preparing for a promotion at work by studying chapter 2 of an applicable manual, but chapter 3 was the material covered on the exam. This would not produce a favorable result—a missed opportunity for a promotion. Pay attention to where your effort is ultimately leading you, so you can reach your intended result: your achieved goal.

Is Your Result What You Desired? Great!

Did you achieve your desired result? Great! Celebrate your accomplishment! As you choose another goal, make a conscious effort to see your new goal come to life!

You want to make the right effort to produce what your goal was intended to produce as your result, right?

⇒ Do you need to adjust your effort by revisiting what you decided in steps 1, 2, 3, 4 or 5? If not, proceed to step 6.

Take time to jot down realizations about your result here. What do you remember from achieving this goal to use as motivation for achieving your next goal? Did you take small steps that moved you closer to your goal faster than expected? Since you may have learned some new techniques to reach a goal, use your experience as proof that you have what it takes to achieve a goal. It's a great way to build your confidence.

Notes

Notes

Notes

STEP 6 - Time Limit

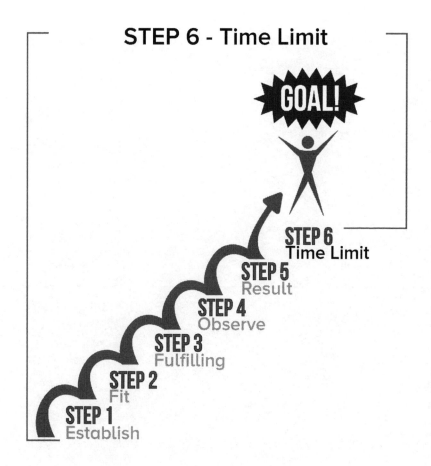

GOAL!

STEP 6
Time Limit

STEP 5
Result

STEP 4
Observe

STEP 3
Fulfilling

STEP 2
Fit

STEP 1
Establish

CHAPTER 7

STEP 6: SET A TIME LIMIT FOR ACHIEVING YOUR GOAL

With no time limit, you could be on a frustrating, never-ending journey. Yes, there may be adjustments to be made. However, the most direct route to your goal will help you maintain an efficient use of your energy and help you achieve your goal in a timely manner. Your result must be tied to a time limit you set, either way.

Give Your Goal a Time Limit

With a specified date to complete your goal, you have a time element that motivates you to continue making an effort. When you set a deadline, you know how near or far you are from reaching your goal. A deadline for a person training for a marathon could be the date of the marathon. A teenager applying to colleges could set a specific date for completing the application process before graduation. A new business owner's deadline for a grand opening could be the first day of the busy season for the industry he or she plans to enter. A travel writer who blogs could set a deadline for releasing a book on the joys of traveling to certain destinations. The release date of the book could be set prior to the busiest travel season, for instance.

Having a time limit means your effort will not be endless. You should have already set a start date as part of establishing your goal in step 1. You also need to know when to expect completion. This gives you a sense that you are moving toward your achievement or it is coming your way soon. After following the six steps outlined so far, you can feel confident you are on the right track. Now, go ahead. Write down the date of completion.

Your end date: _____

Did You Accomplish Your Goal on Time or in Less Time?

Great! Celebrate! As you choose another goal, make an effort to see your next goal come to life.

Has Your Time Limit Expired with the Goal Not Reached?

For instance, if the date of the marathon came and went, and the marathon was not ran, the deadline was not met. If you did not meet your deadline, what effort can you make to adjust your direction now? Is your goal worthy of continued effort at this point? Will you start training for a different marathon or a different type of race?

Take time to write your responses and feelings about the deadline that may not have been met. What does this mean to you? Be honest with yourself. Get to the heart of the matter. Was the deadline unrealistic? Are there other conditions to consider? Were there people who could have helped you meet your time limit? This is information you can use as you make continued efforts in achieving your goals.

Notes

Notes

Notes

Now that you've had time to contemplate what an unmet deadline means to you, decide where you need to focus your efforts. This whole exercise in determining a time limit, in itself, is a fruitful effort toward a goal, isn't it? There is always an effort to be made.

You decide what effort you need to make, and it's okay to deviate from a set path. Your job is to keep making an effort to discover your true direction so you achieve your goals in life with a set time limit. And after you achieve your goal by your set time limit, give your achieved goal the attention it deserves for its continued lifespan. If your goal was to become a professional guitar player and you achieve this goal, keep practicing to maintain your goal's life based on your desire to do so.

A time limit helps you making an effort
that is not endless.

⇒ Do you need to adjust your effort by revisiting what you decided in steps 1, 2, 3, 4, 5 or 6? If not, remember there is always an effort to be made.

What can you take note of as you realize your goal was achieved on time and you start the *Six Simple Steps to Proven Success* process on a new goal? Take time to review what went right and what didn't work out so well this time around. What did you learn from achieving your first goal using this process and you can apply to your next goal achievement? How is that information helpful to you and to others? Reflect on your achieved goal as a treasured point of reference that you can bank on. It will come in handy as a dose of confidence when challenges occur.

Notes

Notes

Notes

CHAPTER 8

HIDDEN OBSTACLES

Are there any limiting beliefs trying to run your life right now? A limiting belief is a thought you've decided is true for you, but it may not be. For the person training for a marathon, a limiting belief could be something like "I'm too old to run a marathon." Even though the person is diligently training, the limiting belief pops up as an obstacle standing between the person and his or her goal. The limiting belief can turn into a load that weighs the person down and prevents him or her from training.

If your goal is still worthy, make an effort to determine how to overcome any obstacles. If your goal is to run a marathon, how about finding a group of runners with similar goals as support? How about adjusting your scheduled training time—or creating a schedule, if you don't have one? You could reward yourself with a relaxing bath after training, which would give you something to look forward to during training. What reward can you apply to your specific goal to keep you motivated to make an effort, if you encounter an obstacle?

Your awareness of a limiting belief gives you the power to take action to overcome it. You have the power to limit the life span of any limiting belief. I read a quote recently that gave me something to think about: *A smooth sea never made a skillful sailor.* Challenges disguised as a limiting belief can actually make us better. We learn to navigate them. Dealing with a limiting belief could actually be a goal to achieve, couldn't it?

If you have any limiting beliefs that are running wild, question them. Seek help capturing and dealing with them. Investigate them.

Some limiting beliefs that popped up while I wrote this book were, *You have never written a book. What could you possibly know?* I questioned those beliefs and countered with *Others have written their first book. I have to start somewhere. If not now, when?* I was able to move past limiting beliefs and do something. It wasn't always easy to make an effort, but being able to see things differently helped tremendously. How can you counter any limiting beliefs? How can you see a limiting belief from a different view? Byron Katie's book, *Loving What Is: Four Questions That Can Change Your Life* is an excellent source for dissolving limiting beliefs.

May you be successful in all your conscious efforts. May you remember and conquer the *how* in your quest for achieving your goals. The impact of your efforts can be life changing when consciously guided, as you learn how easily and effortlessly your effort becomes when you're in tune with achieving your goals.

CHAPTER 9

Useful Ideas and Sayings to Keep You Motivated and Focused

1. The following is a short list of, what I call, *effort affirmations*. You can use them as mantras. Use them to keep you focused during your journey to completing your goals. They rhyme, which makes them easy to memorize so you can easily repeat them if you need motivation from time to time.

When I make an effort toward what I want to be,
I feel my goal already here within me.

If I make an effort to adjust my goal's strategy,
it helps me make my goal a reality.

When the effort I make is toward what I believe,
my goal is what I achieve.

2. Use words that resonate with you as your mantra or chant, such as *peace, joy, love, happiness, abundance, calm, focus, relax, prosperity, faith, breathe, wisdom, thank you, yes, compassion, forgive.* What word or phrase works for you?

3. Complete any small task that may be quietly distracting you from giving your full attention to making an effort toward your chosen goal. Small tasks like, making that phone call to your child's teacher, paying a bill that may be close to overdue, or making the appointment to put the car in the shop for maintenance. That one small task could be a hidden obstacle. It could slow you down from giving your best during the precious time you have allotted for working on your goal. Watch out for them. Be aware. Sometimes it's the little things that will trip you up and rob you of your full attention to your

goal. Clear your path of any small task that may be lurking as a stumbling block.

4. It may not be comfortable or easy reaching out for assistance. However, people need people. We are all connected. You are not alone. If you share your ideas with someone who has total disregard for honoring trust and integrity, it could be very discouraging and damaging. But imagine sharing your goal with someone that is deserving of your ideas and goals. The connection could be uplifting for both.

5. If you keep trying and making an effort, is there really any failure? Or is it just a case of making adjustments where necessary?

6. Searching for things to be grateful for and finding humor even during challenges are great tools for maintaining a level of optimism and confidence.

7. A couple of effort related quotes:

    Success is dependent upon effort. (Sophocles, Ancient Greek Playwright)

Much effort, much prosperity. (Euripides, Ancient Greek Playwright)

8. The world is absolutely waiting for you to share your special gifts in the manner that you express your unique self. No one is capable of doing this but you.

9. Bottom line, find what works for you. Find what motivates you to help you to keep making an effort.

CONCLUSION

For your convenience, here is *How Will I Achieve My Goals?: Six Simple Steps to Proven Success* at a glance.

Step 1 – **Establish** what your goal is and why you want it.

Step 2 – Determine whether your strategy **Fits** your goal.

Step 3 – Determine whether your goal is **Fulfilling.**

Step 4 – **Observe** your progress in achieving your goal.

Step 5 – Measure the **Result** of your efforts.

Step 6 – Set a **Time Limit** for achieving your goal.

One word in each step is the main focus of that step. The first letter in each of these words spells the word EFFORT. EFFORT is a main ingredient in achieving your goals:

Step 1 – **E**stablish
Step 2 – **F**its
Step 3 – **F**ulfilling
Step 4 – **O**bserve
Step 5 – **R**esult
Step 6 – **T**ime Limit

The six-step process supports you each step of the way and can be used as your personal and mobile accountability partner, providing you with ideas and motivating you as you pursue your goals. It can keep you focused on what you need to do in a timely manner.

Only you control your effort. Your effort is the energy you own that moves you through your life. As you make an effort time and time again, you have the power to transform your effort to reach amazing goals. You get to choose. No one can act for you. The one person that has the biggest impact on your decision to make an effort is *you*. *You* alone.

AFTERWORD

It has been a life-changing experience for me to complete this book because it serves as confirmation that achieving a goal can take many twists and turns but still come to life. Being grateful for every twist and turn was a way of seeing every event along the way as a blessing and as necessary to achieving my goal.

I used the concepts in this book to realize my goal of finishing this book. It is a dream of mine to help and encourage others to live an amazing life by realizing they already have what they need to start and finish a goal.

But how? was always a haunting thought for me. Once I decided to make a conscious effort by taking action to start writing, all kinds of help showed up, and things began to flow in an effortless way. Right people. Right resources. Right on time. It all started when I genuinely decided to move confidently toward my goal. Yes, there were stumbles along the way, topped with moments where I felt I was stuck in quicksand, but the *how* showed up right on time...with the effort I made. A perfect example of everything falling into place right on time is when I needed help with setting up social media. Since I didn't know much about how to set up social media or maintain it daily, this is partly why it was scary to me and caused delays. Right on cue I met Yasaman 'Yas' Azarpajouh (in person), a multiplatform media strategist! Turns out, she is a life coach and studied in the same program as I had. We met at a life coaching event and promised to keep in touch. We kept that promise and she is heaven sent. My social media angel. I am comfortable discussing any social media issues with her and she makes it so easy. I had no idea we would be connected in such a way. Things will work out when you make an effort to act on your dreams, goals, and ideas. You will find your 'Yas' right on time.

My efforts served as my unspoken but active faith that I deserved and could accomplish my goal. Change sometimes happened in an instant, and things began to flow. The whole concept of making an effort unfolded. Now my prayer is that you find in these pages the support, encouragement, or guidance that speaks to you to live fully by achieving your goals.

Do you have an inspirational theme song, poem, movie, book, person or group to talk to, or affirmation to recite, or write in a journal? Remember to use whatever you need to stay inspired.

Did you know that your real riches are the ideas you are blessed to have, and you decide to make an effort to bring them to life?

The saying, the journey of a thousand miles begins with one step by Lao-tzu, Chinese philosopher and noted author of the Tao Te Ching; makes it clear that an effort of making just that one step had to be made to achieve the thousand mile journey.

Matthew 7:7—"Ask, and it shall be given you; seek, and ye shall find; knock, and it shall be opened unto you" (KJV); it is clear that this bible scripture indicates that one must make an effort to ask, to seek, to knock before anything happens.

Wishing you the best in all your efforts.

Email Address: reginacarvercoaching@gmail.com

Website: www.reginacarver.com

ACKNOWLEDGMENTS

There is no way I could have completed *How Will I Achieve My Goals?: Six Simple Steps to Proven Success* without help from countless people. Thank you to each and every spirit that I was blessed to interact with or learn from; the comment from the stranger, the encouragement from a song, the billboard that appeared with the words I needed to read, right at that moment … the list is endless.

Special thanks to Debera Khalid. You influenced my writing, my friend. (I bet you didn't even know that.) I love you, and I'm coming out there to visit.

Fonda Jones, my sister, thank you for all those countless accountability conversations and nudges to finish. I love you and thank you for all you do.

DeWitt Little, you are always encouraging, no matter what ideas I dream up. You are always ready to be my guinea pig. You are the model friend. I love you for that.

Susan Green, thank you for your input! Who knew?

Camille Finklea, what inspiring talks we've shared! I enjoy those talks and look forward to each and every one to come. Waiting on your book now. ☺

Verneka Smith, you are wise beyond your years. You amaze me. Thank you for giving me feedback, straight with no chaser. LOL. I look forward to reading your published poems.

Jadwiga Drelich, see what all those texts helped to produce? They weren't in vain. What a pleasure to know you. Thank you!

My deepest heartfelt and loving appreciation to my family and all my friends. I love you all. You have contributed to who I am, with all my perfect imperfections.

I extend gratitude to the Balboa Press staff for being on this journey with me.

May you all have continued overflowing blessings and success, and embraced by love and peace forever!

RESOURCES

Finding Your Own North Star: Claiming the Life You Were Meant to Live by Martha Beck

The Gifts of Imperfection: Let Go of Who You Think You're Supposed to Be and Embrace Who You Are by Brené Brown

Discover the Power Within You: A Guide to the Unexplored Depths Within by Eric Butterworth

Creative Visualization by Shakti Gawain

You Can Heal Your Life by Louise L. Hay

Loving What Is: Four Questions That Can Change Your Life by Byron Katie

The Four Agreements by Don Miguel Ruiz

The Game of Life and How to Play It by Florence Scovel Shinn

Success Through Stillness; Meditation Made Simple by Russell Simmons

The Power of Now and *A New Earth: Awakening to Your Life's Purpose* by Eckhart Tolle

Tapping the Power Within by Iyanla Vanzant

ABOUT THE AUTHOR

Regina R. Carver is a Certified Life Coach. She set a goal of writing a book to inspire people to discover their own answer to "How?" after setting any goal. Her dream materialized as this simple, inspiring guide, *How Will I Achieve My Goals?: Six Simple Steps to Proven Success.* She is passionate about transformational life coaching and enjoys helping individuals break through beliefs that hinder their progress in accomplishing their goals. This is her first project, with more inspiring work to follow. She loves a fun and adventurous road trip. Originally from Benton Harbor MI, she currently lives in Illinois.

24674171R00076

Made in the USA
San Bernardino, CA
02 October 2015